HOPE
A Partner
To Faith

HOPE
A Partner
To Faith

by

Charles Capps

Unless otherwise indicated,
all Scripture quotations are taken from
the *King James Version* of the Bible.

09 08 07   25 24 23 22 21

HOPE- A Partner to Faith
ISBN10: 0-89274-396-4
ISBN13: 978-0-89274-396-4
Copyright © 1986 by Charles Capps
P.O. Box 69
England, Arkansas 72046

Published by Capps Publishing
P.O. Box 69
England, AR 72046

HOPE
A Partner
To Faith

Now faith is the substance of things hoped for, the evidence of things not seen.

Hebrews 11:1

Faith is the substance of things, but hope is a necessity. Sometimes people say, "You don't get anything by hoping." And that's true to a certain extent, for there is no substance to hope.

But hope is a very important partner to faith. Hope is the goal-setter. **Faith is the *substance of things hoped for.*** The substance of "things" — what things? The things you **hoped for**. What do we hope for? We hope for the things that God has given us.

That's why the Bible says in Hebrews 11:6, **But without faith it is impossible to please him.** God is not pleased when we don't enter into the provisions that He made for us. Some things we will never enter into except through faith. God's willingness is multiplied to us through the knowledge of God. We must know what God has given, or we can't have faith in that promise.

> **Grace and peace be multiplied unto you through the knowledge of God, and of Jesus our Lord,**
>
> **According as his divine power hath given unto us all things that pertain unto life and godliness.**

2 Peter 1:2,3

Hope Is Necessary

Hope is a partner to faith. You are reading this book because you hope to receive some insight into hope and faith. But hope alone will not give you that insight. Yet, if it wasn't for hope, you wouldn't have opened this book.

When the sick come into a prayer line, they hope to be healed. If they didn't have hope, **they wouldn't come for prayer.** Since faith is the substance of **things hoped for**, then **there must be some hope,** or there wouldn't be anything for faith **to give substance to.**

This will explain to you why some have died, even though they were saying all the right things. Others say, "I just don't understand why they died." It could be that they gave up hope.

God's Word Gave Hope to Abraham

Look at what Abraham did when there was no hope.

(As it is written, I have made thee a father of many nations,) before him whom he believed, even God, who quickeneth the dead, and calleth those things which be not as though they were.

Who against hope believed in hope, **that he might become the father of many nations; according to that which was spoken, So shall thy seed be.**

Romans 4:17,18

When there was no hope, Abraham believed in hope. There are people today who have no hope **medically**. Doctors have done all they can do. When the doctor says there is no hope, do what Abraham did: **go to the Word of God and get supernatural hope.** He decided to agree with God. That's what we are doing when we make a decision to confess the Word of God. We are coming over to God's point of view by saying what God declared about us.

Some might say, **"There is no hope, so you might as well give up."** You can **always** go to the Word of God and get some hope. I don't care if it's physical, financial, or spiritual. When your situation **seems** to be hopeless, go to the Word of God. God's Word is hope for you.

Hope is a goal-setter. You must have a goal. If you don't set any goals, or if you don't know where you are going, then **how will you know when you get there?** How long will it take you to get there? You don't know where you are going, and you don't know how to get there, but a goal gives direction.

Faith is the substance of things **hoped for. There must be some direction of faith.** Some have said, "Well, I'm just waiting on God. I'm believing God."

Some of those people have been waiting for years, and they haven't done anything. They are not waiting on God — God has been waiting on them. They have made a decision by doing nothing.

When there was no hope, Abraham decided to believe in hope. **He made a decision** to believe God's Word. That is where his hope came from — the Word of God. Don't try to use faith where hope should be, and don't try to use hope where faith should be. **Hope has no substance.** Faith is the substance of the thing hoped for.

So there must be **faith and hope.** They are partners. They go together. **Faith is the divine energy of God.** It comes by hearing God's Word. It is the substance **of things** desired.

We must learn to sow the seed of God's Word. Words are seeds. We speak the Word of God — the promise of God — into our hearts, and it springs forth and grows up: **. . . first the blade, then the ear, after that the full corn in the ear.** In Mark 4:28, it was established by Jesus that the heart was the production center. Jesus called it the soil.

7

Revelation Comes by the Spirit

We talk about the heart being the production center, and Paul adds some light to this subject in his first letter to the Corinthian church.

> **But as it is written, Eye hath not seen, nor ear heard, neither have entered into the heart of man, the things which God hath prepared for them that love him.**
>
> **But God hath revealed them unto us by his Spirit: for the Spirit searcheth all things, yea, the deep things of God.**

1 Corinthians 2:9,10

Eye hath not seen, ear hath not heard. How many times have you heard people quote this scripture and say, "You never know what God is going to do." But **you will know,** if you read verse 10, *But God hath revealed them unto us by his Spirit.*

He is telling us that these things won't enter into the heart of man through the natural five-senses realm. You cannot get revelation knowledge into your spirit through the five physical senses. But **God reveals things** to us by His Spirit.

God's Spirit bears witness with our spirit and reveals by revelation knowledge that we can't get any other way. God will do everything He said He would do. God will do everything He promised. **He will do everything you believe Him to do, if your faith is based on His Word.** But these things have not entered into the heart of man through the **natural eye** or the **natural ear**. They entered into the heart of man by revelation. God has revealed them to us **by His Spirit**. God **did** reveal them, but not through the five physical senses.

God has an avenue through which He reveals things and sometimes it bypasses the carnal mind. God reveals things to our spirit by the Holy Spirit. He is our teacher and guide.

The Human Spirit Searches

In 1 Corinthians 2:10, both uses of the word "Spirit" are capitalized. The first part of the verse says, **But God hath revealed them unto us by *his Spirit***. This is referring to the Holy Spirit. But where it says, **for the Spirit searcheth all things, yea the deep things of God,** that is not referring to the Holy Spirit. That refers to the human spirit — your spirit. Proverbs says it this way:

> **The spirit of man is the candle of the Lord, searching all the inward parts of the belly.**

> Proverbs 20:27

The human spirit is the light bulb that God uses to enlighten you. God's Spirit beareth witness with your spirit. God's Spirit bears witness with our spirits and enlightens our spirits.

For *the spirit* searcheth all things, yea, the deep things of God. I believe the Apostle Paul is referring here to the human spirit, for the Holy Spirit does not need to search the things of God. The Holy Spirit already knows the things of God. **It's the human spirit that searches the things of God**.

When you are asleep, the seeds you have planted in the heart are producing. And you don't really know how. All you did was sow them, and go to bed and get up.

Your Spirit Knows — God's Spirit Knows

For what man knoweth the things of a man, save the spirit of the man which is in him? even so the things of God knoweth no man, but the Spirit of God.

1 Corinthians 2:11

God's Spirit knows all about God, and your spirit knows all about you. If you get your spirit in contact with God's Spirit, **you have tapped the source of all knowledge.**

Now we have received, not the spirit of the world, but the spirit which is of God; that we might know the things that are freely given to us of God.

1 Corinthians 2:12

We need to connect this with what Paul said in verse nine. **Eye hath not seen, nor ear heard,**

11

neither have entered into the heart of man, through the natural five senses.

You didn't see it by the physical eye, you didn't hear it with the natural ear, but God revealed it. It came by revelation of the Holy Spirit into your spirit. **The spirit searcheth all things, yea, the deep things of God.** So, after you **sow the seed into your heart,** while you sleep at night, **your spirit searches for the wisdom and revelation of God** in regard to ways and means to bring that seed to production.

Then you will wake up some morning with an idea that came from the Spirit of God into your heart, and you won't know when or how it came.

Verse 12 states that **God gave us the human spirit** so that He could reveal the things of God to us.

> **Which things also we speak, not in the words which man's wisdom teacheth, but which the Holy Ghost teacheth; comparing spiritual things with spiritual.**

But the natural man receiveth not the things of the Spirit of God: for they are foolishness unto him: neither can he know them, because they are spiritually discerned.

1 Corinthians 2:13,14

Comparing Spiritual Things

We must compare spiritual things with spiritual. The spirit of man contacts the Spirit of God to find revelation knowledge of these things concerning our everyday lives. We don't gain revelation knowledge through the carnal mind. It comes into the human spirit.

The natural physical body does not receive the things of the Spirit of God; but the things of the Spirit of God are received into the human spirit, which is the production center.

But he that is spiritual judgeth all things, yet he himself is judged of no man.

1 Corinthians 2:15

Who is **he that is spiritual**? Now, remember, he said to compare spiritual things with spiritual. He that is spiritual judgeth all things. The part of you that is spiritual is the inner man or the spirit. Your spirit judges all things.

Your human spirit may pick up things about other people that you do not understand with your natural mind. It has not been revealed to you through the eye or the natural ear or any of the five senses. At times, you sense some things and you don't know how you know, but you know that you know that you know.

Enlightened by Your Spirit

You may meet someone and it seems as though your spirit says, "Get away from them. Don't have anything to do with them," and you don't know why. Your spirit will draw up in a knot. Your spirit was "searching all things," and it found something and was warning you.

He that is spiritual judges all things, but he himself is judged of no man. Your spirit **senses** something about the person's spirit, but you yourself cannot **judge** what is in their spirit. You can only judge their actions.

> **For who hath known the mind of the Lord, that he may instruct him? But we have the mind of Christ.**

1 Corinthians 2:16

We gain the knowledge of the mind of Christ by the Holy Spirit, through the human spirit.

The spirit of man truly is the light of the Lord. Let's put these two thoughts together. In Mark 4:26, the heart of man is referred to as the soil. It is where you plant the seed of the Word of God so it can produce.

It is the Spirit that reveals things to you and gains the knowledge. **God has given us His Spirit so that we might receive the things of the Spirit of God.** The heart is the reception center.

When you speak words, you are sowing seed. When you are speaking the Word of God, **you are sowing incorruptible seed.** That seed will not fail. Yet it is possible for your action or inaction to cause a harvest failure. The seed will not fail. But what we do with the seed could cause a production failure.

Slothful Man Prophesies His Own Doom

In Proverbs 22:13, we find this statement:

The slothful man saith, There is a lion without, I shall be slain in the streets.

The slothful man is one who isn't going to do anything. He just sits there and says, "I'll be eaten." He doesn't even run. He could at least make an effort to get out of the street. **But he prophesies his own doom.**

Those who don't act on the Word of God are doing that all the time. They say, "Well, you know, we're all going under." "Nothing ever works out for me." "The world's going to blow up in one big atomic blast, and we're all going to be doomed." The slothful man prophesies his own doom.

Natural Things Reflect
Spiritual Things

We are capable of conceiving God's Word in our spirit, bringing forth production of what God said in His Word. Remember, hope is a goal-setter.

Sometimes, when we see these things in the Bible, we tend to take them completely out of their natural setting. When Jesus talked about sowing a seed, He didn't take it away from the soil and say, "This is a spiritual thing."

We make a serious mistake when we totally separate the natural from the spiritual. God's Word is spiritual, but it works like a natural seed. The heart of man is spiritual, but it works like natural soil.

Let me give you an illustration of how the heart is designed to produce. Let's bring it down to the natural level where we can all understand it. There probably is a piece of equipment at your house called a heating and air conditioning unit. It is the heart of the heating and cooling system.

That unit has been designed by an engineer to control the temperature of your house. That's all it was designed to do. It is designed to produce whatever you dial into that little thermostat on the wall, which we will call a goal-setter. The heart of that unit was designed to produce whatever temperature you dial into that thermostat.

The numbers on that thermostat represent degrees of temperature. Let's say it is 100 degrees outside, and you want the temperature to be 70 degrees inside. Your job would be to turn that goal-setter to 70 degrees. As long as it is kept on 70 degrees, **that unit will work night and day to see that the goal is reached.**

You wouldn't have to fast and pray that it would get cool in your house. The unit knows how to do it. That is what it was designed to do. You would simply dial the goal-setter, and it would send an impulse to the heart of that unit and say, "Get us some cold air in here. It's hot." With the thermostat on 70 degrees when it's 100 degrees outside, you have created a problem for the heart of that unit. But it can handle it. That is all it knows to do, but it can do it well.

That unit won't wash your clothes, it won't cook your dinner, it won't clean your house. It wasn't designed to do those things. It was designed for one purpose: to produce what you have dialed into the goal-setter.

The Heart Produces

Now let's relate this to the heart of man. The heart of the heating-cooling unit is like the heart of man. **You must set the goal for the thing you want produced.** Faith is the substance of things hoped for, and hope is the goal-setter.

Hope works in the head. What you continue to speak becomes your goal. Your head is the goal-setter. When there is no hope, there is no goal set for the better — although "no hope" sets negative goals.

Like the thermostat on the wall, your spoken words send an impulse into your spirit.

By saying, **"In the name of Jesus, by His stripes I am healed. I am redeemed from the curse of the Law, and I forbid sickness and disease in this body,"** you set your goal on healing.

What are you doing by that action? Someone may say, "You are lying, because you are sick." You may be sick all right, but the purpose of speaking God's Word is to set your goal and plant seed. Some people don't understand how you can say you're healed by the stripes of Jesus when you are hurting. But you must decide to establish that goal regardless of present circumstances.

Let's relate this concept to the way a thermostat works. Let's say it is 90 degrees in your house, and you come in and turn the thermostat to 70 degrees. Someone might say, "Hey! You can't do that. That's a lie. It's not 70 degrees in here."

But it's not a lie. That's the way to make the heating-cooling unit work the way it was designed. That's the reason you set it on 70.

You are calling for that temperature. You are calling for the temperature that is not manifest. That is the way the system is designed, and that is the only way it will work. If you set 90 degrees in the thermostat when it is 90 degrees already, there will be no change. The unit will remain inactive, producing nothing.

The Heart Is True to Demands Placed On It

Surely no one would be foolish enough in natural things to argue with you when you turned the thermostat to 70 degrees. But they will when you set your goal on God's promises.

Some will argue that you are lying. You have to give some time and meditation to these things to fully understand the design of the heart (spirit) of man.

It's easy to understand the way that goal-setter (thermostat) works. By looking at this example, it's easier to understand that faith and confession work that way on your heart. You may not believe it works that way. You may not like it, **but that's the way it works.**

No one would argue with you about turning that thermostat to achieve the desired temperature, and no one would call you a liar. They understand that it will be 70 degrees in the room in a few minutes.

The heart (spirit) of man is like the heart of that heating-cooling unit. It is designed by God to produce the very thing that you plant in it. You plant it or set the goal by speaking it.

When you first hear your voice on a tape recorder, you usually think it is someone else. You can't believe it is you, because you have been hearing your voice mostly with your inner ear. Your voice is picked up by the inner ear and fed directly into your spirit.

When you heard your voice on the tape recorder, you heard it for the first time totally with the outer ear and could not believe it was you.

God designed you that way, so your voice would feed the impulse of what you desired right down into the garden spot, the heart, which is the soil. (Luke 13:18,19.) There it will produce what you are speaking. It is also renewing your mind as you are confessing God's Word.

Suppose someone turns the thermostat to 70 degrees and then, in a little while, they turn it to 95. Then they turn it to 60. It will not work properly that way. It will probably blow a fuse. It is not designed to be flipped from one extreme to the other all at once. It will blow a circuit.

Someone might say, "Who would be dumb enough to do that?" Christians do that all the time. They start making faith confessions: "Glory to God, my needs are met according to His riches in glory by Christ Jesus." They say that for a few days, then they look at circumstances and say, "Dear God, it's never going to happen. We will never get these debts paid. I don't know what we are going to do."

Well, they just changed the thermostat. You have to set it where you want it and leave it there. That unit will work day and night to produce what you have dialed into it. It will never argue with you.

The Unit Does Not Make Decisions

Have you ever heard a heating-cooling unit say, "No, I'm not sending cold air; you need hot air, so I'm lighting up the fire to send you some heat"?

If it did that, we would have to say, "Well, you never know what that unit is going to do. It has a mind of its own."

But it doesn't work that way. It is consistent. It always produces the very thing you call for, and that is how the heart (spirit) of man is designed.

> **The spirit of man is the candle of the Lord, searching all the inward parts of the belly.**
>
> Proverbs 20:27

Thou shalt also decree a thing, and it shall be established unto thee: and the light shall shine upon thy ways (path).

Job 22:28

Mark 4:26 tells you the way it works. It is as if a man cast the seed into the ground. That is setting the goal. A seed to a farmer is a goal-setter. If you want to know what goal you have set for your garden, just look and see what seed you have planted. You plant the seed, and it works. You go to bed and get up. You don't have to hope to God that it will work. It will work because it is designed that way. The substance is in the seed itself.

Thermostats Have No Substance

Suppose someone who had never seen a thermostat or a heating-cooling unit saw you turn the thermostat to 70 degrees when the room was 90 degrees. When it began to get cool, he would wonder why it was getting so cool. He would want to know what you did.

"What is that little box on the wall?"

You say, "That is a thermostat."

"A thermostat. Where can I get one?"

You see what he has in mind. He goes down to the hardware store and buys a thermostat. He goes out to his cabin and nails it on the wall. Then he turns it to 70 degrees and sits down and waits.

He will have a long wait, because the goal-setter does not have the ability to cool his cabin. It is only a goal-setter. There is no substance in the thermostat to cool a room. Yet it establishes a goal to be met.

Faith is the substance of things hoped for. Let's say it another way. Faith is the substance of everything needed to accomplish the goal hoped for. That cooling unit has electricity connected to it **and is available at any time the thermostat makes a demand on it.**

That heating-cooling unit won't produce anything by itself. There must be a goal-setter, and you must dial the goal. Hope is a goal-setter for you. Always speak your hope.

Your goals for your heart are set by speaking those things in faith. Whether the unit feels like it or not, when that thermostat's impulse goes to that unit, it releases the energy that is available, and it immediately starts producing the thing you dialed into it.

Your Hope Makes Demands by Being Spoken

That is the way the heart (spirit) of man works. You take the Word of God, and you speak it. You set the goal. The divine energy is in God's Word to cause the heart to produce. Even in the summertime, the energy that is bringing forth cool air in a building is the same energy that brings hot air in the wintertime.

The goal-setter (your hope) **is the thing that determines whether it is hot air or cool air.** If you're not satisfied with the harvest you're getting, **check up on the goal you're setting and the seed you're sowing.**

27

That unit won't argue with you. It's not designed to decide whether it's right or wrong. It's only designed to produce whatever you call for.

The heart of man works that way. Speaking the Word sets the goal. We have so separated natural things from spiritual things until most people believe there is no relationship between them. But Jesus brings them back together when He says, **If ye had faith as a grain of mustard see, ye might say. . .** (Luke 17:6).

Then in Genesis chapter eight, God says:

> **While the earth remaineth, seedtime and harvest, and cold and heat, and summer and winter, and day and night shall not cease.**
>
> Genesis 8:22

The Bible keeps referring to sowing. You sow the seed, you reap a harvest. Whatsoever a man soweth, he shall reap. That's the way it works.

The soil in your garden doesn't decide whether or not what you plant is right or wrong. **The soil will produce whatever you plant in it.** Some believe that the human spirit, or the heart, of a born-again person would not produce anything bad. But ask yourself this question, "Why do some people backslide and go back into sin?"

Jesus said it this way:

> **A good man out of the good treasure of the heart bringeth forth good things: and an evil man out of the evil treasure bringeth forth evil things.**

Matthew 12:35

I am convinced from what Jesus taught that even a person who is born again can put evil things in his heart. God considers anything that is contrary to His Word to be evil. (Num. 13:32.) James said it this way:

> **If any man among you seem to be religious, and bridleth not his tongue, but deceiveth his own heart, this man's religion is vain.**

James 1:26

In other words, your tongue can deceive your heart.

The Soil Never Argues

I was a farmer for 30 years before I went into the ministry. Never in all the years that I farmed did I plant soybeans and hear the ground say to me, "We aren't going to raise soybeans, we're going to raise cucumbers and bananas," because the soil has no choice but to produce what is planted. Hope causes you to speak your faith.

But some have gotten the idea that it doesn't matter what they sow and it doesn't matter what they say. "Well, God knows what I meant," they say.

Would you say, "I planted radishes, but the soil knew what I meant; I meant to plant tomatoes"?

Certainly not. No one would be that foolish in the natural. You would know you were not going to raise tomatoes, because the soil doesn't produce what you meant but what you planted.

The soil of your heart does not decide whether what you plant (say) is right or wrong. Its job is to produce the information needed to cause what you are saying (planting) to come to pass, whether it is right, wrong, or indifferent.

Mark 11:23 is not a one-way street. But Jesus only told us how to operate faith on the positive side. He didn't want us to operate the principle on the negative side.

> For verily I say unto you, That whosoever shall say unto this mountain, Be thou removed, and be thou cast into the sea; and shall not doubt in his heart, but shall believe that those things which he saith shall come to pass; he shall have whatsoever he saith.
>
> Mark 11:23

Another Way to Say It

Believe that those things you sow will come to pass, because the saying is the sowing.

The goal is to be set on removing the mountain or the tremendous problems you face. Your hope then will cause you to speak your faith. On the other hand, it will work just as fast on the negative side. Some say, "This mountain is getting bigger every day. I'll never get over it."

They are right, because they are working confession of faith on the negative side. It will work just as quickly — and sometimes quicker — on the negative side.

Some prophesy that "Things are getting worse. We'll never make it. We'll never pay our debts. We'll never get this church going." They have no hope, so there is nothing to which faith can give substance.

They are speaking that into their soil (heart). It will cause their spirit to search the avenues of God's wisdom to find a way to bring it to pass.

Remember, the unit won't decide whether you need heat or cold, it only responds to the signal sent from the goal-setter. *Hope is the thermostat for your heart.* If you have no hope, no impulse is sent to the heart, and there will be no positive production.

Even though there is substance in the heart (faith), without **hope** there is no positive goal. **Hope causes you to speak the promise. Fear causes you to speak the worst of everything.**

Remember, it is not going to work just because you say it, but saying it is involved in working God's principle, and it will eventually produce the results God promised.

Several years ago, when I saw this truth, I started confessing, "I am redeemed from the curse. In the name of Jesus, I forbid sickness to operate in my body." At that time, I had ulcers. Every so often, I would be laid up for two or three days a week and couldn't do anything. I drank Maalox by the bottle.

Then I started confessing the Word of God concerning my healing. Over a period of about three months, the Word of God was engrafted into my spirit and the ulcers left my body. They tried to come back a few times, but I would say,

"No, in the name of Jesus, I have received my healing." I am healed. I am well. I am delivered from the curse of sickness. I continue to resist sickness like I resist the devil.

Conception Necessary Before Manifestation

I learned how to operate in these principles through trial and error. I made some mistakes, but I continued to confess that I am redeemed from the curse.

I confessed, "I am redeemed from poison ivy." But when I came into contact with poison ivy, it would get on me. Just about every time I went deer hunting, I got poison ivy. Someone said, "Your confession is not working, is it?"

I would reply, "Yes, it's working. Faith is coming; faith is coming."

I was setting the goal. I kept confessing it. What happened? I got poison ivy again!

What did I do? I put Calamine lotion on it, and it dried up. Then I continued to confess the Word. This happened several times before the manifestation came. It took time to conceive the Word in my heart and cause faith to come.

Faith in the heart gives it the ability to conceive God's promise. Once it is conceived, you will eventually have a manifestation of that promise.

I continued this for about a year and then noticed that poison ivy didn't affect me anymore. The corresponding action that I had toward what I believed was that I continued to confess it, even though natural circumstances said that I was not redeemed from it. I just kept saying what God's Word said: "I was redeemed from the curse, according to Galatians 3:13 and Deuteronomy 28:61."

God's Word Is Over All Matter

Some people say, "That is mind over matter!" But it's not. **It's faith in God and His Word over all matter.**

When it was conceived in my spirit, it manifested itself in my physical body. At first, if I had said, "I am going to have full corresponding action toward what I'm saying and pull poison ivy off the trees with my bare hands," I would have been in trouble, because I was just beginning to set the goal and sow the Word into my heart.

I didn't have full corresponding action toward what I was saying until I had the full manifestation. After about a year, poison ivy didn't affect my body. Now **I can have full corresponding action toward poison ivy.** My skin does not react to it. But it took about a year to conceive God's Word to the point that Galatians 3:13 was manifest in my body.

These things are not going to happen overnight. But they will happen, if we are diligent to agree with God and confess what He said about us.

Confession Is a Process

Confession of God's Word is a process of renewing the mind. It causes faith to come. It is an expression of your hope. The heart conceives the promise you are speaking and brings the manifestation. This is the way it works in your physical body, in your finances, and in other situations of life.

But it takes time. It is a process. This is not a fad. This is a way of life. This is not something you try. If you are just going to try it, it won't work for you. If I had been trying it, then the first time I got poison ivy, I would have said, "It doesn't work." But it never occurred to me that it might not work, because Jesus had said that it would.

Practice Increases Production

Once you have found these Bible principles, study them and practice them. Don't back off from them when things appear to get worse. Just stay with it and confess it until it develops inside you.

That doesn't mean that you wouldn't use medicine, if it's necessary. Yes, I used Calamine lotion. I took Maalox and everything else I could find to keep the symptoms down until I received the manifestation.

Don't come under condemnation because you take medicine. So many allow the enemy to condemn them for that reason. Don't let anyone force you into trying to operate on their level of faith **if you are not developed to that level.** Medicine won't heal you, but it will keep the symptoms under control.

Let's say it this way: **Medicine won't heal you, and it won't keep you from *being* healed.** Remember: **Faith and hope are partners and you need them both.**

Start where you are. Use some common sense. Operate on your level. Confess God's promises daily. Your faith will grow and your productivity will increase.

Books by Charles Capps

Hope - A Partner to Faith
Seedtime and Harvest
God's Image of You
Success Motivation Through the Word
The Tongue –A Creative Force
Releasing the Ability of God Through Prayer
Can Your Faith Fail?
Changing the Seen and Shaping the Unseen
God's Creative Power Will Work for You
Authority in Three Worlds
How You Can Avoid Tragedy
Angels
Hebrews Syllabus
Faith and Confession
Substance of Things
How to Have Faith in Your Faith
Kicking Over Sacred Cows
The Light of Life
God's Creative Power for Healing
Jesus Our Intercessor

www.charlescapps.com
or call
1-877-396-9400

Charles Capps is a retired farmer, land developer, and ordained minister who travels throughout the United States sharing the truth of God's Word. He has taught Bible seminars for twenty-four years sharing how Christians can apply the Word to the circumstances of life and live victoriously.

In the mid '90s the Lord gave Charles an assignment to teach end-time events and a revelation of the coming of the Lord.

Besides authoring several books, including the bestselling *The Tongue, A Creative Force*, and the minibook *God's Creative Power*, which has sold 2.8 million copies, Charles Capps Ministries has a national daily syndicated radio broadcast called "Concepts of Faith."

For a complete list of tapes and books by Charles Capps, or to receive his publication, *Concepts of Faith*, write:

Charles Capps Ministries
P. O. Box 69
England, AR 72046

Feel free to include your prayer requests and comments when you write.